Sleekit: Contemporary poems in the Burns stanza

SLEEKIT

Contemporary poems in the Burns stanza

edited by **Lou Selfridge**

Published in 2024 by Tapsalteerie
Tarland, Aberdeenshire
www.tapsalteerie.co.uk

Cover art: *Kat met muis*, Cornelis Bloemaert (II), c. 1625.

ISBN: 978-1-7384396-2-1

Printed by Imprint Digital, UK

Katie Ailes's poem 'To Us' was commissioned by Glenfiddich for Burns
Night 2022. 'The Gellick' by **Stephen Dornan** first appeared in *Irish Pages*
Vol.6, No.2 (2010). 'Chiefly in the Scottish Dialect' and 'Tae a Sex-Toy' by
Harry Josephine Giles were first published in *The Games* (Out-Spoken
Press, 2018). 'An Epistle' and 'To a Moussaka' by **W.N. Herbert** were
first published in *Omnesia - Remix* (Bloodaxe Books, 2013). 'Ode tae a
Hose-Fish' by **David Kinloch** first appeared in the anthology *New Poems,
Chiefly in the Scottish Dialect* (Polygon, 2009). 'The Working Birds' by
Simon Lamb won the Robert Burns World Federation's International
Write-A-Habbie Competition 2021 and was first published in *When the
Universe Creaks* (self-published, 2021). 'Sapphohabbies' by **Iain Morrison**
was first published in *makar/unmakar* (Tapsalteerie, 2019). And **Stewart
Sanderson**'s 'Love's Labours' Won' was first published in *An Offering*
(Tapsalteerie, 2018).

Introduction • Lou Selfridge

Sleekit republishes a selection of twenty-first century poetry in the Burns stanza (by the likes of David Kinloch, W.N. Herbert, and Harry Josephine Giles) alongside a number of new poems in the form by some of the most exciting poets writing in Scotland today. Included here are poems which conform to the rules of the Burns stanza alongside poems which seek to stretch and twist the form; poems in Scots, English, and JavaScript; poems on topics as diverse as Buffalypso, sex toys, and Robert Burns himself. The work included in *Sleekit* shows the vital role the Burns stanza plays in contemporary Scottish poetry.

• • •

What, however, *is* the Burns stanza? Also frequently referred to as the Standard Habbie or Scottish stanza, it is the form in which many of Robert Burns's most well-known poems are written, including 'To a Mouse' and 'Address to a Haggis.' The stanza is formed of six lines of varying lengths: it begins with three long lines, followed by one short line, another long line, and a final short line. All the long lines rhyme with each other, as do the short lines, giving the rhyme scheme *aaabab*.[1] All this is made

---

1. For the pedants, a more technical definition of the Burns stanza:
The four *a*-rhyming lines in the stanza are each iambic tetrameter, and the two *b*-rhyming lines are iambic dimeter. The flexibility of English-language metre means that these lines can be hypercatalectic (having one additional syllable tacked on to the end) – something which Burns does

much clearer by looking at the opening stanzas of Burns's 'To a Mouse,' which shows a standard use of the form:

> Wee, sleekit, cowrin, tim'rous *beastie*,
> O, what a panic's in thy breastie!
> Thou need na start awa sae hasty,
> Wi' bickering brattle!
> I wad be laith to rin an' chase thee,
> Wi' murdering *pattle*!
>
> I'm truly sorry Man's dominion
> Has broken Nature's social union,
> An' justifies that ill opinion
> Which makes thee startle
> At me, thy poor, earth-born companion
> An' *fellow-mortal*!

The stanza, though technically complex, has produced some of the most memorable poetry in the Scots language; indeed, it is the form's intricate DNA which lends it so well to memorisation, with its persistent rhyme and lilting music producing earworm stanzas.

• • •

Many of the rules of traditional poetic forms (such as the sonnet, the sestina, and the villanelle) have been stretched

---

frequently. Don Paterson also argues that 'the dimeter lines have two perceptible ghost metrons [a.k.a. silent feet]' (*The Poem: Lyric, Sign, Metre*, [London: Faber & Faber, 2018], 531); I tend to agree with him on this.

and broken by poets over time; those using traditional forms in the twenty-first century are particularly enthusiastic about bending the rules to suit their own poetic project. Take, for instance, the sonnet, a form which has been loosened over the centuries to such an extent that any fourteen-line poem (and many thirteen-, fifteen-, and sixteen-line poems) can be categorised as a sonnet. Rhyme and metre, if not quite made irrelevant, have become non-essential components of the contemporary sonnet. The Burns stanza, however, is not open to quite this degree of flexing and stretching: the highly specific rules of the stanza mean that any serious deviation from them risks producing a poem which is formally unrecognisable.

This is not to say, however, that poets are not interested in pushing the limits of the Burns stanza; experimentation with the rules of the stanza can be seen in much recent work in the form. Maria Sledmere, for instance, abandons the Burns stanza's rhyme in her poem, 'Tapering,' but retains its variable line lengths.[2] This gives us stanzas such as the following:

> Our pharmaceutical meetcute
> will scintillate future windfalls
> taking their sweet time inside the
> same arteries
> a likeness shot in heart
> multiples of

---

2. Sledmere's metre is more syllabic at times than stress-based, but the lines retain a similar – if not identical – outline to the traditional metrical outline of the form.

Life hearts from the inventory
leaving us spent and cordial
to have fought the open morning
for you my love
who turns such sentences
to ardent dares

Sledmere's engagement with poetic form resembles the Burns stanza, but can it truly be categorised as a poem 'in' the Burns stanza? And how far can the stanza be stretched before it goes beyond recognition? Similar questions are raised by Craig Aitchison, who retains the stanza's rhyme but abandons its metre in 'Gaun':

It's no fair.
Ye're no there.
Onywhere.
Gane.
No that A care.
Gan oan.

Whether such poems are 'in' the Burns stanza is for readers to decide; it may indeed be the case that such poems are 'beside,' 'around,' or 'against'—rather than 'in'—the form. Such experimentation, however, tests the limits of the Burns stanza, contributing to the life of the form in contemporary poetry.

•   •   •

The Burns stanza has seen somewhat of a renaissance since Douglas Dunn's statement, in a 1997 essay, that 'it is some time since a Scottish poet' used the form.[3] Leading Scottish poets, including W.N. Herbert and Harry Josephine Giles, have contributed to a revival of the form in the twenty-first century, and some of their finest works in the Burns stanza are republished here. This is a critical moment in the Burns stanza's revival in contemporary Scottish poetry, and this anthology tries to capture a snapshot of the poetry currently being written in the form.

Although most famously connected to Robert Burns, the stanza has roots long before him—examples can be found as early as medieval France and thirteenth-century England.[4] Since Burns took up the form, however, it has largely been under his dominion, and many poets writing in the stanza post-Burns have had to contend with his legacy. Janette Ayachi's 'Robert Burns in Scottish Stanza' and Harry Josephine Giles's 'Tae a Sex-Toy' both present a challenge to Burns's masculinist domination of the form and of Scottish poetry more broadly. There are also many vibrant parodies of Burns's most famous poems—with W.N. Herbert's 'To a Moussaka' and David Kinloch's 'Ode tae a Hose-fish' riffing gleefully on some of his most well-known lines. Such poems show the continuing significance of Robert Burns to contemporary poets in Scotland, whilst demonstrating a playful reaction against

3. Douglas Dunn, 'Burns's Native Metric', in *Robert Burns and Cultural Authority*, ed. Robert Crawford (Iowa City: University of Iowa Press), 83.
4. Allan H. MacLaine, 'New Light on the Genesis of the Burns Stanza', *Robert Burns Chronicle* (1954): 48.

the icon-status he is often elevated to. Contemporary Scottish poets aren't afraid to take the bust of Burns off its pedestal and kick it about: hardcore Burns stans may find such subversion unsettling, but it shows his lasting involvement in a living poetic tradition.

Not all of the poets writing in the stanza are directly interested in Burns, however, and it is heartening to see poets applying the form to subject matter as diverse as QAnon (in Kate Tough's '(To a) Nous') and blue tits (in Simon Lamb's 'The Working Birds'). The Burns stanza, in the hands of these highly skilled contemporary poets, seems capable of holding just about any content. Unlike the narrow sentimentalism of many earlier poems in the Burns stanza, these poets explode the traditional confines of the form, flooding it with contemporary concerns and applying it in new and unpredictable situations. Harry Josephine Giles's 'Chiefly in the Scottish Dialect,' for instance, is composed by applying a Markov chain algorithm to the works of Robert Burns, whilst Calum Rodger's 'arcadia.js' is written in JavaScript, a programming language.

All of the poets in this anthology have taken the Burns stanza and, in one way or another, made it new. They prove the versatility of the form, illustrating in vivid terms its continued relevance to poetry in Scotland and beyond. Their engagements with the Burns stanza are often sleekit, slippery, and sly, but the results are thoroughly exciting.

• • •

This anthology was supported by the Sloan Fund at the University of St Andrews, which encourages the writing and publication of Scots-language poetry.

There are many people without whom this book would not exist. Thank you to Duncan Lockerbie at Tapsalteerie, for taking on this project and nurturing it with such care; to Laura Cameron-Mackintosh and Alex Bain at the University of St Andrews, for kindly assisting with the administration of funding for this project; to all of the poets published in *Sleekit*, for entrusting us with your poems; and to Aarushi Malhotra, Sachairi Nixon, Fraser and Jenny Selfridge, for generous guidance along the way. Finally, this anthology *really* would not exist without the support it, and I, have received from the outset from Dr Peter Mackay. I am most sincerely indebted to him, for everything.

Lou Selfridge, St Andrews, 2023.

To Us • Katie Ailes

Whene'er guid fowk in kinship meet
An men their neebors kindly greet
In harmony oor glad herts beat
Wi joy an mirth
To gaither is the gift maist sweet
Upon this earth.

Roond kitchen tables chattin late
Or dancin halls wi gracefu gait
Whate'er we've come to celebrate
On ony nicht
Cross centuries to congregate
Is purest bliss

For ilka man's a single strand
O thread, but noo by clasping hands
We mak a fabric 'cross the land
Fae coast to coast
Sae noo let's aw thegither stand
An raise a toast

Tae us! To us! To all of us, all gathered here
In spirit, body, and good will
No matter where our journeys take us
Our souls are bound together still

And even though the world keeps turning,
Turning dawn to deepest night,
Turning seeds to flowers bright,
And turning seas to deserts dry –

Yes, even though some oceans smoulder,
Cresting waves baked into dunes,
The land an arid, barren plain,
All foam blown into shimmering sand –

Yes, even still we have each other
We always have – we always will
In loyal kinship, joy and trust
O dearest family, here's to us.

Faw • Craig Aitchison

It gaithers mass and steidy wechtens,
all aroond cloods thicken, mirken;
burthen growes, it jeels an boukens
tae rain or snaw,
noo cleeks an sae its brichtly skinkin.
An doon it faws

free frae baunds tae huad it there,
wun oot fae a gresp that held it sair,
fawin free; crimp clauchts nae mair,
nae tack at aw,
drapping, skiftin throu the air
it faws an faws,

fawin throu dag an drowe an blae,
doon throu steuch an smuir an gray,
doon taewart a great stramash A gae
but doon A faw,
tae whitever weird A'm fawing tae
A faw an faw.

Gaun • Craig Aitchison

It's no fair.
Ye're no there.
Onywhere.
Gane.
No that A care.
Gan oan.

Are ye tho aye?
You said aye.
Mine forby.
Gane.
Aye, but juist stay.
Gan oan.

Robert Burns in Scottish Stanza • Janette Ayachi

A diet of women, wine & song
What could possibly go so wrong
This is the place where I belong
& I love it
It bulks me up & makes me strong
Fuels me with grit.

I speak in stardust, incantations
I dress in silk & selkie skins
& I confess all my near sins
To the whole world
Where I end & where I begin
Is one big swirl.

Baritone of my bones sing heavy
Beneath the belly of my bevvy
I reach for life that feels fleshy
So I can sleep
Legend & myth just like Nessie
Into the deep.

With romance, friendship, food & drink
One is always allowed to think
Most things to music we can link
Words to lyric
This is how we stop the near sink
It's generic.

From couch to ceilidh, up you get!
No rest from the workers sore head
It won't be long before we're dead
Let's celebrate
With throats open wide to be fed
If that's our fate.

My role, I speak for my people
Escape societal shackle
Make folk laugh, bellow & cackle
Like the stars say
I'm Aquarius, I mingle
In lots of ways.

Most mornings I work the farmland
It's my duty to give a hand
But my health is taken like quicksand
The elements
Rake their toll against all I planned
In settlement.

I am restrained from who I love
So breed as wide as a turtle dove
Migrating to fields from above
I know these roads
Journeys that give the words a shove
Like breath, they flow.

Hemlock, porcelain & then smash
I weary myself back from crash
Marry my love under lightning flash
Father unleashed
Allowed now to follow my stash
For all such peace.

Kids & animals catch my heart
I've always known this from the start
Losing my daughter, the worst mark
Death has ingrained
After this stopped the morning lark
I live in pain.

Seasons come fierce, I watch from my room
Try not to let myself hug gloom
My tooth is removed more ache looms
So much is lost
I crawl to my horse left ungroomed
Dip into frost.

I trust my friend, dear physician
Wide cabinet of medicines
Each one a trick from the magician
Ripe sorcery
To sip with my broth of venison
Soon I'll be free.

I drink from the well, dip in the sea
But want to stay in bed with whisky
The delirium knocks my family
All to the still
Too late now for my recovery
I've had my fill.

Chronic illness & infection
My heart's walls go up in correction
The water too cold to section
Any more time here
Live fast, die young; a quick reflection
Nothing to fear.

I've left my brood my legacy
Many women mourning after me
It's no wonder I'm not left in peace
Long after rot
To unravel any mystery
Least not forgot.

I live on, I play on the souls
Of many from where heather grows
& beyond as life does unfold
Each year I'm sung
On my birthday I rise & roll
Kiss winter sun.

The Gellick • Stephen Dornan

Ah bide in neuks the lee-lang day
An rear my thrangs o weans away
Fae comfort, heat an licht o day
Sprattlin in clart,
Whaur ceevilisation haulds nae sway,
Nor polished art.

You dinnae like tae think Ah' m here,
Aboot your sonsy, fauncy gear
An gin you see me sprattlin near
It's batterin broom,
Or stampin shoon, Ah doubt an fear
Will seal my doom.

Ah'll exercise my muckle hooks
Amang your claes an unread books,
An stick my neb at nicht fae neuks
Crawlin and creepin;
Then, wi steady feet and furtive jooks,
Ah'll find you sleepin!

Doon your lug hole Ah'll come dashin,
Borin, burrowin, batterin, bashin
Hokin, wigglin, garravashin,
Intil your heid
An lae you sneezin, pechin, fashin,
Wi oot remead.

Like an ammonite concealed in stane,
Ah'll curl richt up and bide my lane
Atween your gullet and your brain
An hibernate;
Ah'll dormant bide until your pain
Micht dissipate.

Like an arraheid ablow the glaur
Or a peat-choked body buried far
Ablow a bog Ah've unco power,
Like artefact or relic;
An whan Ah twitch sic wurds Ah'll gar
Spew fae your bake as 'gellick!'

To a Buffalypso • Roshni Gallagher

Buffalo sailed over the sea
with only waves for company
and man made the new and mighty
      Buffalypso!
Swaying by the cashew tree
      Buffalypso!

Beast of burden, Buffalypso –
a crown around your head. Laid low
by work and human to and fro –
      singing calypso.
Now, even the moon's soft glow
      singing calypso.

Loping beast of muscle and mud
in the fields and up to no good
your cloven hooves and horns misjudged
      like a devil's!
Sharp bone that could draw fresh blood
      like a sickle!

And corralled under contained skies
your voice a bellow or a cry –
your time is brief. Hold your head high!
      Your gentle life.
Sadness in your soulful eyes,
      your lonely strife.

But beast of beauty, strength, and pride
over fields, with the sun, you stride.
The mango trees on the hillside
    singing calypso.
The wind and the shifting tide
    singing calypso.

And running swiftly in your herd,
magnificent as the water birds
that fly with you. There are no words
    Buffalypso!
In you, beast and myth are blurred
    Buffalypso!

Chiefly in the Scottish Dialect • Harry Josephine Giles

Knot ss ss sak: Thigirrutl Gond!
Be pusl but kimso bomarct,
Zinaly ye bis torndanyoghe,
      Dau sosorv care,
Wap horns: aro alo oplk put,
      Tig bran wowepple.

As trorcavand gromess gbo id;
Thaple withe e'er her ha wings
Opriter'd crong onfumeles face,
      In the you.
Mud le! Qushe sen te ma wht shoad,
      Heeaylsmyeul.

Sthe yo he's fonere prt liabr!
Or be I pounitates, smee!
Burop thas fet snd sulik samat
      Atheenenly qun,
Wi' tisht scowontredrapr handon
      D boowifaldd.

Her bend ae blos, I've auld him wize
The that e's of Deasuree previle
Stan' lemned mout her place ing samer
      Just funere Mouse,
Wi' simpletonor Grese, thath aff
      Upow'riouste.

He neer tol made an' Saun but worder
But them and par to fathem slaw;
His thine! Rightes abonna now,
      Or wi' as st.
Low stim'd, whate had, a fe's shantrave
      Tho'er IN WEE.

Ye leart an' sets yet you, Tillocknie,
We's to this they'll Withe dom nanes chot;
An' sooth ew'd biel pa ught bank hast
      Somer's pleat,
He'll laight a dudding bosome coals,
      Warms oss measure.

The sweet in could-like offer cracks,
Thou pay't to fable in sic a man's
The Thou lad ye can youthful flame
      In tenting growth;
My fant aff care to arch, great head:
      I visage Enjoyme.

The pinest Lore I cantranger metter,
Her sure foul represert ye thirring,
Mome days your play: ye can tho' bred,
      I lock, I mars?
Ev'n thou their lord the pointed Mice
      Vaint Scotlang's are us!

When loween a slee, and ye the tide out,
But tent up an' prawl, an it earth
For soupleasure the gainstreams
    The rascal may engage;
Gaed heart the wad na flight an yet
    UPON WEE, stow!

Some merry drink they better were
Yon mixtie-maxtie, quiet an' caups
When upward cam up, hap-step-an'-loup,
    As lang's the graces;
Ye hum away amang the win's;
    There's sic a lunt.

Or if I slumber, fancy, chiel,
As ill I lisp an' wines to gie,
But, Thou art good, and then Goodnight,
    To reach selfish end;
My dearest of distill, your dear,
    In Mailie dead.

But thou, ALL-GOOD, for some SCOTTISH MUSE
In thae auld wife's flainen toy;
Or frosts on hills of Ochiltree
    Are hoary gray;
Or blinding drifts wild-furious flee,
    Dark'ning winter season.

O Thou wha gies us each guid gift!
Gie me o' wit an' sense a lift,
Then turn me, if Thou please, adrift,
      Thro' Scotland wide;
Wi' cits nor lairds I wadna shift,
      In a' their pride!

Tae a Sex-Toy ● Harry Josephine Giles

Wee sleekit, tirlin, purpie buttplug!
Come here n gie yer yaupie slutbug
a keek at hou like ony smut-drug
       ye cheenge wir warlds;
come in, faw til: wi doucest nut-tug,
        wir tale unfurls...

O buttplug, whan ye're in ma rectum
A'm plucked as true as string by plectrum,
baith corp n pith as an electron's
       baith point n wave;
ye appen up a pleisure spectrum;
       ye mak us crave

a life whaur aw o thaim wi prostates
(or ither glands) whit want an onwait,
whas langsome sex-lives anely frustrate
       thair carnal needs
hae easins appened tae bullets, cock-mates
       n anal beads.

Fer ken ye nou, for aw that sex is
but wan ploy in the offensive
for liberation o wir feckless
       fair fowk n planet,
it's swank, it's snell, it's that infectious
       scads canna staund it.

Wad that wir heroes haed yer glamour!
Gin Rab the Bruce n Ed the Haimer'd
kent hou ye'd reduce tae stammers
      the gabsie makar,
wad than wir nation yet be daumert?
      wir history knackered?

Sae picture nou gin Willy Wallace,
a laird as macho as wis gallus,
took as his ettle no the phallus
      o sword set swingin,
but insteid a puckered anus
      aw ripe fer rimmin.

Haed Wallace just haed ye, vibrator,
fer tae gie insteid o claymores,
wad he n Langshanks than hae catered
      tae ilk ither's lust?
wad rose n thistle hae masturbated
      til baith war dust?

Or think again, did Bonnie Charlie,
feartie feck, the wan at hairdly
kent the fowk at he sent chairgin
      while he was leggin,
get the arsewark lacked sae sairly?
      did Flora peg him?

We ken the Brave kent well submission,
but no wi safewords or that fission
o bed fae body in positions
       o hole surrender:
dear buttplug, wad ye tak the mission
       o New Pretender?

A've lost ma drift… Ma theory's this:
that Scotland's happit in manly myths
whit grieve fer aw at's lost, at's missed
       by defeatit glory,
but a Scotland sheuk wi anal bliss
       is anither story.

An, tho the yarn's mair raivelt yet,
whan homonationalism's set
tae neutralise wir queerer threats
       tae queen n country,
whan creative agencies beget
       a salmagundi

o pink poond-chasin fads n fashions,
makkan aw wir slaurie passions
nocht but capital, but cash-ins
       on rebel grief,
whan roond ma sex-toys is that ashen
       haund o deith,

in spite o aw they monolithic
forces reenged tae quell the mythic
pouer o duntin up yer rovick
        a godemiche,
A'm sure wi anal play wir civic
        dwaum's unleashed!

Aye, aiblins rectal activism's
reproductive futurism
in ither guise (cruel optimism
        tae want for mair),
tho but tae shift tae butts fae jism
        is fankelt fare:

tae big utopia up yer shitter
says awbody's a counterfeiter
wha's juist wan wey tae win the fitter
        an lichter life
the futur's bright n clart wi skitter
        baith saught n strife.

Gin failure's queer, sure Scotland shoud be,
fer wha's like us at failin? Naebdy.
Insteid o waily-wailin, coud we
        no celebrate
the gender rubble o this bluidy
        failed state?

An gin the rectum's grave, A'll bury
thare ma sel, ma state o worry;
A'll touch n feel ma wey tae blurry
　　　　non-duality;
if naething else, A'll sup the slurry
　　　　o pure venality.

A ken that mair self-penetration
willnae really end aw nations,
or buttplugs spring th'emancipation
　　　　o wir common weal,
but thay are pairt o the liberation
　　　　fae deid ideals!

for tae ken yer anal passage
is tae win a better vantage
on the bonnie, quirky marriage
　　　　tween gie n tak,
tap n bottom, tent n ravage,
　　　　free n brak.

Aye, whan A haud ye, buttplug purpie
as a thistle, A feel worthy
o a nation doun n dirty
　　　　wi buried treisure!
o a warld at's free! n thirsty
　　　　fer filthy pleisure!

Sae, Jacobites n Forty-Fivers,
drap the Saltire, wheesht the piper,
wash yer haunds, relax yer tichter
       orifices
n let yer buttplugs be the drivers
       o aw wir wishes.

An Epistle • W.N. Herbert

Leeze me on rhyme! It's ay a treasure,
My chief, amaist my only pleasure
– Burns

While London's steekit beh thi snaw
and ilka sleekit chitterin jaw
       is ettlin tae describe
hoo drifts ur white, and ice is cauld,
and feel thi lave maun be enthralled –
       Eh've Bowmore tae imbibe.
And as the nicht – mair dreh nor me –
       draas in, Eh think Eh'll scrieve
a wee epistle tae, let's see,
       thi deid and Doctor Grieve –
          auld hermits, wee MacDiarmids,
             thi ghaist o guid Lapraik:
          here's a ravie fur young Davie,
             and a rant fur Rabbie's sake.

For the tartan telephone is playin
'Fur Auld Lang Syne'; some cloud's displayin –
well, it's no quite the Batsign – weans
       wull hae nae clue,
but aa thir dominies are prayin
       tae Burns's Ploo.

Some anniversary or ither
huz gote thi lot tae plot thigither
and ask frae whaur – Stranraer? – or whither
        remeid sall come:
they've caaed aa gowks fur blinks o blether
        baith deep and dumb.

In stately manses Haggismen
puhl sheeps' wames owre thir heids and then
descend beh greenie poles tae dens
        whaur desks await;
they raise thir stumpy Haggispens
        and smear on slates.

While maskless weemen keep ut edgy
an gee wir man a retro-wedgie –
remind us hoo his views got sketchy
        on burds and… beasts;
demand thir haggises be veggie
        and, glorious, feast.

And aa the waant-tae-bes are Robins
mair willin tae wark hard than Dobbin
and fuhl o antifreeze fae bobbin
        fur bacon rinds –
thir beaks, aa chipped, let slip thi sobbin
        of achin minds.

Thi anely time that Scots gets read
is when thi year lukes nearly dead –
          it seems tae need extremes;
when winterin leaves are lipped wi frost
and wolf-pack winds pursue the lost
          and ink, in deep freeze, dreams.
When Naichur jinks yir toon's defence
          and bursts yir comfort's net
wi snaw fitbaas, then tae thi tense
          come wurds thi waurm furget:
                    deep-layerin, like swearin,
                         we dig oot attitudes;
               wi stanzas come answers
                    tae city pseuds and prudes.

Whit Burns wiz sayin tae Lapraik
wiz whit we are's eneuch tae make
a puckle lines that salve life's paiks:
          we need nae ticks
nor teachers' nods, nor critics' shakes –
          we're no that thick.

Ut's no that anely crambo goes
that jingles oot, jejunely, woes:
Burns claims he disnae ken whit's prose,
          whit's poetry,
but see hoo crafty his rhyme flows,
          and braid as Tay.

Whit Burns bethankit Davie fur
wiz freenship in thi dargin dirr:
when, pure ramfeezelt, thochts gae whirr,
      tae knock back gills
by ithers' ingles, bields fae smirr,
      can stave aff ills.

But here Eh sit wi midnicht's nip,
or leh doon whaur thi verses slip,
or rise tae brose and habbies' grip
      aa oan ma tod,
neglectin meh professorship,
      in the nemm o Gode!

Fur twenty fehv years – mair – Eh've trehd
tae scrieve in Scots and it's nae leh
that billy's gone – sae why deneh
      Eh've ootlived Burns?
Fae Davie tae Lapraik we fleh
      wi nae returns.

Ootlived, but no ootwritten yet,
nae superbard, nor Guardian pet
      nor whit maist fowk wad read;
tho fit fur (no sae) prehvut letters
wi a dictionair sae crossword-setters
      micht love me when Eh'm deid.

But whit Burns foond inben oor speak's
        a glede fur aa McSlackers:
gin Doric's heat is kin tae Greek
        Eh'll scrieve 'To a Moussaka.'
                And thi ithers? Jist brithers
                    and sisters eftir aa:
                still-hopefu peers and hoped-fur feres –
                    Eh think thi ink micht thaw...

To a Moussaka • W.N. Herbert

Moussaka, multistorey prince
of scoff – furst aubergine then mince
then tatties tappit wi a chintz
          o bechamel –
ye gift fae Greeks that brings on grins
          jist beh yir smell.

Pagoda o thi denner table,
as tooers gae, an anti-Babel,
ye mak the universe feel stable –
          wan tongue wull pass
fur taste and toast: let aa wha's able
          creh oot '*Yia mas!*'

Some noodles claim *Pastitsio*'d
win ony prehz – no in this ode;
nor *Kleftiko* can steal thi vote
          nor *Soutzoukakia*:
let them that miss oor dish's boat
          wear *Papoutsakia*.

There's some prefer ye cut fae trays,
some baked in pottingers o clay,
some add courgettes and some say nay –
          but aa agree
thi furst true taste o Holiday
          can anely be...

Moussáka! – said as amphibrach
tho that micht mak a Cretan lauch:
it shid be cretic here, but, ach,
      whit's *Moússakás*?
Ah'm fae Dundee, sae in meh sprach,
      nae use at aa!

But Eh've plenty o rhymes fur a guid *Moussaka*
far mair nor Greece huz financial backers –
did Clytemnestra, husband-whacker
      hae as mony whacks?
Constantinople rank attackers
      lyk this at thi Sack?

– as mony as forks besiegin *Moussakas*
wieldit beh genius or beh jackass,
Kazantzakhes or some *vlakas*
      aa shiftin amoonts –
ye'd need an abacus (or jist Bacchus)
      tae haundle thi coont.

Sae be an archaeologist
o appetite, dig thru its crust
and nose thi *nostimáda* – mist
      o history;
this Byzantine wee treisure kist
      that aa can pree.

Thi Padishah wad dine on this,
thi Doge gee his lasagne a miss,
thi Emperor bestow a kiss
        upon uts cook:
its pages spell a book o bliss,
        come tak a look –

or tak a moothfu, rich and reamin –
then sing, ye weel-contentit weemen,
since Eh, fou-stappit, faa tae dreamin;
        sing oot, ye masters:
hud Troy a horse filled wi this daimon,
        it'd faan faur faster!

Yia mas!: (Greek) to us!;
vlakas: (Greek) blockhead;
nostimáda: (Greek) tastiness.

Ode tae a Hose-fish • David Kinloch

Big, slochie, fliskie, braisant beastie,
Bluid fae three herts stirs thy breastie!
Twa pumps yer ginnles, an wan yer feisty
      Green-blae copper hide!
Echt airms an suckers sook the tasty
      Paella fae the tide.

Research has shawn yer gey mair mensefu
Than the fowk wha clock yer high IQ;
A Heidegger o molluscs, you
      Fill the airy
Bane aneath yer raucle skin bung fu
      Wi buoyancy;

The buoyancy o bein here,
In this warld o sand, buccaneer
O Fush whase flauntie rump's as queer
      As this Scots leid.
A Houdini o chromatophores
      Your inky screed.

The sillersmith howks oot yer rainbow
Bane. It muilds the jowels on trousseaux
O hures an maiden aunts, puir pseudo-
      Bijouterie.
Yer calcium's fur parakeets low
      On charivari.

Your Cubist een are miracles
O organogenesis, wrinkles
At swag back an fore an signal
            'Vive cephalopod!'
Gin this leid wiz hauf as souple
            Then I'd be God!

But Hosie cries oot: 'Aye, it is!
It is, it is, it is, it is!
Gin it can mak "rime riche" wi "is"
            – there's anely five –
Ye'll ken the standard habbie's fizz
            Is still alive!'

The makar swalls wi pride tae think
Hermetic verse is no extinct
His wurds a hauf-way-hoose, a kink
            O fush an scaup.
This leid's no deid, it's in the pink!
            The great auk's talk!

A livin watergaw o sea
An bane, yer sepia dye's a key
At polarises, then fricassees
            The beach's licht:
Sunlicht's these wurds ye speak tae me,
            A second sicht.

The Working Birds • Simon Lamb

We watched as blue tits built their nest
this spring within our garden, blessed
to sit as architecture's guest
  from dawn till gloam,
as day by day they strived and stressed
  to build a home.

They worked with unrelenting zest
to find and fetch and craft their best,
till king and queen puffed-up a chest:
  Now we belong.
They paid to be our garden's guest
  with nowt but song.

With that, we thought the tits would rest,
but one kept zipping on a quest:
a feathered streak, a bird possessed.
  We knew the score:
what once had been a two-bird nest
  would soon be more.

And sure enough, as we had guessed,
the space within the box compressed,
when sharp and shrill and unrepressed
  new songs were sung
that split the sky, the silence wrest:
  the cry of young.

Such to- and fro-ing from the nest
left us breathless and impressed
to watch the parents' greatest test:
        to raise their own.
Another morsel to digest
        atop our throne.

The weeks slid by and we addressed
a sadness we could both attest
that soon we'd host an empty nest,
        sans songs, sans birds.
The parting of the ways was pressed
        in air, in words.

And on the day they flew the nest,
we felt a tugging in our chest,
as bird by bird, they bravely blessed
        our patch of blue:
first frenzied flight with helmet crest,
        then gone. Like you.

This autumn, now, we sit and rest
in silence, in an empty nest.
Not sad, just hoping for the best
        for you, our world.
Go fly like blue tits, proudly dressed
        with wings, unfurled.

Sapphohabbies • Iain Morrison

Qu-qu, Qu-qu, Qu-qu-qu, Qu-qu, Qu-qu
Ee-ee, Ee-ee, Ee-ee-ee, Ee-ee, Ee-ee
Rr-rr, Rr-rr, Rr-rr-rr, Rr-rr, Rr-rr
   D-d-d, D-d
i-I, i-I, i-I, i-I-i
a-A, a-A, a-A, a-A-a
rr-Rr, rr-Rr, rr-Rr, rr-Rr-rr
   y-Y, y-Y
mm-Mm, mm-Mm, mm-Mm, mm-Mm-mm
   ee-Ee, ee-Ee.

Think I'm having one of eureka moments?
Your affective take on my first engagement
reads me worst when most it neglects our variant
   modes of expression.
An habit of financial ruin
sees what it opts to see, not heeding
the drag from food or buy-to-let when
   the banks stayed cashed.
Deleveraged, though, reduced commitments
   make gloomy graphs:

how a foot has stood on 2016!
Euro boost we're getting, mind you's surprised with
modest growth apparent across the quarter,
   Russia is shrinking.
A couple of percent's a pain for
exporters stuck at bottom levels,

their cloth is stretched. You'll note the current
        account its weakest,
the worst it's been, if not yet held as
        a stress position.

Output, productivity, what's the difference?
Figured man confronted with daunting noughts, I
felt this morning, moving through airport systems,
        filled with flat lines,
a clouding I wished unconnected
to those in air we somehow met
and swallowed as they lined the skies of
        our aircraft's flightpath,
the trans Brazilian dead, returning
        as apparitions.

Ana Matheus steadily had been posting
as their number neared to two hundred women
killed last year. I broke up my hour and half flight
        mentally adding
as more than one per minute flew through
the tube our storage lockers made them.
We'd only hear their bundled forms as
        they thumped above,
and tense, sure that the doors would open
        in bursts of clothing.

Only forty seconds or so between the
body hurtles, we wondered dimly how our
luggage passed them; still the illusion somehow
        encapsulated

each phantomed body, onetime real.
Exquisite corpse of our reviews
we wondered whether we'd join up
        in what we asked.
Being the cis male respondent
        I felt pushed back.

Mirror, mirror, what would you wish me mirror?
Spoken to as man that's a zero presence,
from the start confess the desire that her book
        alters in writing.
The stage door to the Fringe is open.
I host a play, *Picasso's Women.*
For two weeks actor Colette Redgrave
        and her star Judith
and her star Kirsten strut performing
        their scripted speeches

penned by Brian McAvera, first performed at
National Theatre, Radio 3 conjointly,
Russian Olga, Marie-Thérèse and Fernande
        barter acceptance.
Considers what are right dynamics
of powered men and their relations
to women in the current context,
        a thoughtful play,
so add it to your August list
        and don't delay.

Iain Morris' debut collection *I'm a
Pretty Circler*, tender within its pages
punchy, patterned poems with drag queens in them
  £9.95.
Has also lived and worked in Cambridge,
responsibly commissions poets,
and for the first time you return him
  a book he sold,
which bids him swell on straight mechanics
  of text reception.

Houses stretch their girls on the runway, marking
where your queer security's strained and strengthened.
Love and perspiration, our fight is foursquare,
  here's where it shows
in time, in money, children being
like me anthologized, moreover
I'm read in Orkney, I have photos
  to prove Brazil
and haply by departed loved ones
  in heaven still.

Here's my thought how writing or readings of it
makes, creates community not just content,
read by some, by breathing is spread to others
  out through the stirred world.

Per conta da sensibilidade
An inflammation of the ear
has caused a sensitivity
        that's meant these last days
I go to sleep while listening to
        the pulse my heart beats.

This same inflammation resulted from a
targeted assault on my life. The picture
shows me here in hospital two days after,
        late in November.
With luck recovery continues
and this is my part-healed appearance.
I share the story with you grateful
        we lost not this one,
and stand a-love, a sister put it,
        our best revenge.

Ha-ha, Ha-ha, Ha-ha-ha, Ha-ha, Ha-ha
A-a, A-a, A-a-a, A-a, A-a
Pp-pp, Pp-pp, Pp-pp-pp, Pp-pp, Pp-pp
        Y-y-y, Y-y
nn-Nn, nn-Nn, nn-Nn, nn-Nn-nn
ew-Ew, ew-Ew, ew-Ew, ew-Ew-ew
y-Y, y-Y, y-Y, y-Y-y
        ee-Ee, ee-Ee-ee
a-A, a-A, a-A, a-A-a
        rr-Rr, rr-Rr-rr.

Jan. 2019

Ma Scotland is • Jeda Pearl

whorls o snowdrops refusin tae mope
bluebells convenin unner th oak
a glimmer o fawns wi thair kinfolk
fine legs o birch
sleekit smirr that gies ye a guid soak
willow, like church

low sky gatherin clouds in thair flocks
sparrows squabblin, a cauldron o hawks
starlings swell granite in paradox
larynxes strum
goldhammers – prophets o equinox
wingfuls o sun

bladderlocks n deid man's bootlaces
microcosmic rock pool embraces
coastal melodies – shoreline graces
ripe mussels thieft
gulls screekin, swaddlin wind displaces
salted grief

aye

auld coal cellars wi daddy-long-legs
clamberin tenements, skylight webs
duckin washin lines, hide in hedges
backgreen escapes
skitin doon th hillside oan yer sledge
hail bites, high stakes

tim'rous recitals o cherished Burns
does this poetry deserve ma tongue
sweetened wi cane sugar companion
how we enlighten
imagine oor Rabbie campaignin
for reparations

Scottish surnames across Jamaica
both bonnie lands o wood n water
inherited by twin isles' daughter
witches, mystics
when wi gaun mak equalisation?
optimistic

plenty still reek monies, palms bluid greased
excessive atrocities bequeathed
say yer frae here – thay dinnae believe
brave Caledonia
isnae racist so hud yer truth – wheesht
fearless nation

aye, aw that
but it's

sweepin hills o mauve-turnin heather
gilt-tongued gorse hostin May Day blethers
candied clovers in leesome weather
nettle sent'nels
purple thistles burstin wi feathers
at summer's close

thick cloaks o haar tae hush dour mornin's
lang yairns n fowktales tae courie-in
wry maids o mist, dirges for yearnin
feisty insults
skimmerin wirds soundin oot meanin
land o poets

taps aff for a fleetin wing o sun
endless ceilidhin while th night's young
myndin oor histrae tae mend, atone
skouth, aye enough
reclaimin courage – fearless nation
heavin wi love

arcadia.js • Calum Rodger

Introductory note:

'arcadia.js' is a poem in Habbie stanzas written in code. As
well as strictly following the metrical pattern popularised by
Burns, it also constitutes a working program according to
the logic and syntax of JavaScript, the world's most popular
programming language. Like the bacchanalia it describes
and Auden's famous definition of poetry, however, it 'makes
nothing happen', that is, it performs no meaningful functions
and produces no output. Nonetheless, in the few milliseconds
it takes for the poem to run, a small world of language and
objects is written then erased, leaving behind no trace of its
existence.

On vocalisation of the text:

Symbols listed below should be vocalised as follows:

=   'be', 'is' or 'are', depending on syntax. Exceptions are
        on lines 3, 36 and 42, which should be voiced 'equal' or
        'equals' to meet sense and metre.

+   'plus'

<   'is less than'

>   'is more than'

===   'be' (line 28); 'are' (line 47)

.   'do' or 'doth' according to preference.

Symbols not noted above should not be vocalised, but may in
some cases serve as caesurae.

```
let loose; let joy = "unconfined";
let usLeaveTheWorldBehind;
let habit = undefined;
let debt = null;
let we; for (i in we) {let mind
= "rich and full";}

let microBacchanaliaBe;
let dose = ["music", "moonlight", "tree",
"fellow souls" + "ecstasy"];
while (dose.find(() => {})) {
let bliss = "no hyperbole";
we = "aligned";}

const ant = "life and all its woes";
const rained = "we by daily prose";
const ernating = `our throes,
we crash and burn`;
if (we) {for (i in we) {let go;}
let us; return;}

let poemsSoundLikeSmallMachines;
let programsRunLikeRusticScenes;
let allThatIs = `like our dreams
& free of care`;
for (we in allThatIs) {let seams
= "gin to tear";}
```

```
let here = "garden"; here = "bright";
here = "endless moonlit night";
here = "where we land our flight";
while (here === true) {
here = `where we'll meet, fond sprite,
we'll wait for you`;}

let meetingPlace = null + "beach";
let life = ["apple", "orange", "peach"];
let fruit = "fruit"; life.forEach(() => {
"surrender all";})
let eachTasteRuptureEachBiteBreach
= "ing the Fall";

let nothing = "our guiding star";
let theVoid = "avatar";
let usTakeThingsFarTooFar;
if (nothing <
this) {for (here in arcadia) {
we = "yes";}}

let idyll = ["brief", "happy", "gift"];
if (allThatIs + "all that lifts"
> true) {idyll.unshift();}
let graciousWe;
for (we in nothing === 'we who drift') {
we = 'ergo, we be';}
```

Farai un vers de dreyt nien • Stewart Sanderson

after Guilhem IX of Aquitaine

Ise mak a poem oan naethingness –
Nocht ae masel, ae ithers less,
Nocht youthfu an nocht amorous
        Nor some sic twaddle –
Foond i the airms ae Morpheus
        Upo a saddle.

I dinna ken whan I wis born,
I dinna tak delicht or mourn,
I dinna gang alane or scorn
        An maun bide sae
As ane nicht oan a heich hill's horn
        Decreit a fey.

Gin I'm asleep or wauken, weel,
Ye maun spier at some ither chiel
Anent the whilk I dinna feel
        Ma hairt rax sair –
By Sanct Martial, a moose's meal
        Is worth faur mair.

Forfochten am I, like to dee
But ken naething nae telt tae me:
A doactir I maun shairly see
        But kenna whaur –
Guid doactir gin ma seikness flee,
        Bad gin it scaur.

I hae a fiere, but kenna whae
Fir I hae nivver seen her, nae,
Nor wi her foond lichtness or wae
        But I'm fine single
Sae lang's the French and Normans stey
        Faur frae ma ingle.

We've nivver met, but ma luve's strang;
She nivver did me guid nor wrang;
Nae seein her maks blithe ma sang
        Fir I dae care
Imaginin her aw day lang
        An she is fair.

My poem's duin, its theme unkent –
Tae this ain here I'll hae it sent
An eftir frae thaim oan it's went
        Doon tae Anjou
Ain thair sall parse oot whit I meant
        An send the clue.

Love's Labour's Won • Stewart Sanderson

Unlike the vanished *Hamlet*, this
loss would have been a comedy:
five funny acts, to take the piss
    out of that monster, love –
an ancient vice, like poetry,
    which no one is above.

Pinched from a dog-eared chronicle
picked off the barrows at St. Paul's,
the plot remains untraceable
    though if compelled, I'd guess
that it involved strains, dying falls
    and someone saying yes.

The scene is equally obscure:
a blank utopia no art
of reconstruction can restore;
    a placeless mystery
from which we'll never pluck the heart –
    such is love's victory.

In this void the protagonists
are struck dumb, their soliloquies
consumed by time's entropic mists
    towards whose censorship
all our assumed identities
    inevitably slip.

I picture them: the boy, the girl
played by a boy, the clever clown
who sang and sometimes rolled a pearl
        of rare wit on his tongue –
the troubled head under a crown,
        the duke no longer young.

Two thousand or three thousand lines
of prose and blank verse, pared away
till in the end all that remains
        is three words to remind
people about this missing play
        substantial as the wind.

For all the miles of text his hand
set down, a single speech survives
and six scrawled signatures, like sand-
        grains cast up by the sea:
a clutch of desiccated leaves
        to prove there was a tree.

Not everything he wrote was great.
Even for him, there were off days
when no words could interrogate
        this world which took his son
and, given two *Love's Labour's* plays,
        gave back *Love's Labour's Won.*

Ode tae a Tunnock's Teacake • Gill Shaw

ah eye up thon wee gildit temptress
ken soon she'll let me help her undress –
peel aff her skirt wi practiced finesse
while ah birl her roon
they chocolate curves call oot fur caress
let ma fingers scoon

ah'll cradle her sae she's suspendit
then flip her ower sae she's upendit
an dae whit ah ken she indendit
bite her biscuit aff
ah'll dip ma tongue in – she'll taste splendit
sweet an sticky, saft

ah'll gulp the rest doon in a wunner.
gie up silent prayers tae Tunnock's
but wi her gone ah'll nae be scunnered
caucht up in ma thochts
while it's true that she wis a stunner
ir's five mair in the box

Tapering • Maria Sledmere

Our pharmaceutical meetcute
will scintillate future windfalls
taking their sweet time inside the
same arteries
a likeness shot in heart
multiples of

Life hearts from the inventory
leaving us spent and cordial
to have fought the open morning
for you my love
who turns such sentences
to ardent dares

Emotional billionaires
on snow day ceaselessly smaller
who wants to make an angel of
the end of their
internet history
sleepy precious

Cannot fathom empathy for
the ethical privilege of
being maximalist anon
on my shoulder
a sell-out wild as speech
shoves into me

No sex picaresque forgiveness
losing my only friends to life
as it happens to make itself
cyanosis
of untrust choir covers
us in muses

To nurse and totally perfect
these marketing initiatives
we target at rainbows to be
okay I swear
on my insomnia
give us this head

Long stare in sun and sheltering
by formal lily pool, lover
you should know better than to love
after all what's
left is the sluice of
unmentionable

Fierce value titration of clouds
insufflating a poor god song
in the gentle skull of sister
my therapist
said try keeping a book
of your soft grief

I just wanted stimulants, my life
to be alone in the darkest
all its ever known, myrtle climbing
homegrown spine of
colourless lustre, like
no one, nowhere

Parenting the seed we planted
deep in what can't be ours, time-blind
diffusing its labour to a
chest pain, the same
cost watering to death
in my own bed

Will start to beget more brain fog
tried everything to tell the crowd
of leaf-blown anorgasmia
for poetry's
occupational hazard
I will save you

SYMBØL • Taylor Strickland

sauchiehall is scalded loss. hey-ho.
grecian fronts. towers. bay windows.
Mackintosh library burnt to tosh so
      i walk a mock-shell.
once celebrated high street. now low.
      now lower. oh well.

sauchiehell passes for nightlife. no.
the willowless lengths to which i go
go nowhere like. minging Mango.
      SYMBØL. Taco Bell.
i shadow folk who fall. hirple home
      as their shadows still.

on sauchiehall i befriend álvaro
de campos. the next day wave hello.
from across the road he shouts hello
      as the universe. falls
into place outwith ideals or hopes.
      there on sauchiehall.

Lauders • Taylor Strickland

ah *mo charaid* he calls me. calls me
my pal in gaelic having learnt some
gaelic myself we practically rhyme
       sitting together
outside Lauders. me nursing my dram.
      he his tawny port.

warmest summer. arms summer-warm.
he said everything has become a dream.
thuirt e. chan fheàirrde mi na fuaim.
      said i'm no more
than a noise. a voice you yourself hum.
      the wind discovers

that through the empty chair beside me
dust dispersed can flesh out his vacuum
of air. the way the swirl on my thumb
      leaves its spectral mark
bare when i set down the crystal stem.
      my faint signature.

McLellan Works • Taylor Strickland

fire after self-fuelled fire
eviscerates this late fallacy
of a city. yet McLellan Works
       catches by surprise.
with its blonde neoclassical expanse
       & cupola's rise.

we meet for one final coffee.
he laughs. lisbon shares with glasgow
delusions so ordinary
       they pass like place
names through your reflection. in the train
       window. a presence

glassy as certainty.
nothing matters if nothing exists.
i never studied engineering.
       não vivi aqui.
never lived here. nor did you. when we meet
       again let it be

on some impossible plane. lisbon.

(To a) Nous • Kate Tough

Those who can make you believe absurdities
can make you commit atrocities. — Voltaire

The first who tried to convince me
of QAnon's brand of idiocy
was a white male Brit in his sixties
who lived alone
and worked alone, in 2019.
> (I was viewing his dead mum's house as a rental but
> it still looked exactly like a dead mum's house and
> he seemed unstable so I didn't rent it.)

The second one who tried was ditto –
a male white Brit who lived-worked solo.
'You'll change your mind about Trump!' he bellowed.
I dragged my bags
out of his taxi, 'No I won't!'
> (We'd disagreed about pussy-grabbing being a sign
> of poor character. 'What if Trump had grabbed *your*
> daughter?')

The other two were 60s women.
Both white, retired, single living.
In 2020, '21
a lockdown text
that Katy Perry eats the young.
> (Then Hogmanay, where a woman wanged on about
> imminent, major Democrat arrests which, of course,
> never materialised.)

Aye, this is not a (proper) habbie
against the seniors or the solitary.
It's a lament and it's a plea
for common sense;
employing critical faculties.
   (And reducing internet time spent mainlining theodicy
   involving the now ex-president of another country.)

How naive do you need to be
to read Q's dumps and yet not see
a ruse that is derisory?
Oh! Use your nous!
Trump rids us of child trafficking?
   (If that least racist very stable genius was ridding
   the world of anything he'd be the first to claim
   full narc credit.)

Such handy cover for a lifelong creep;
a pageant pest, a pal of Epstein.
Ivanka perched upon his knee,
fourteen in age,
with her hand cupped to caress his cheek.
   (And him later telling The View that he'd date her, if
   he wasn't her father. *A troubled life? A troubled family?*
   Looks can be deceiving, observed Q, about a Biden.)

Of all the men to venerate
Q picked the one in a deep state
of elite, entitled callous hate

who mocks disability
and females' appearance excoriates.
    (In 2017, *Dear Patriot. God is with us.*
    SATAN has left the WH. Oh? Popped out for golf?)

Q'ers rage against fake news and yet
believe whatever Q confects
without demanding evidence
or giggling at
themselves – it never seemed far-fetched?
    (*Why is this relevant?* Is asked on repeat.
    Research for yourself. Think for yourself.)

'Cause it was never breaking news
that governments don't tell the truth,
more is the fool who thinks they would.
Alas, Q'ers
there is no logical follow through
    (that because your leaders are less than honest ergo
    you can take at face value any old porridge posted
    online).

Yes, social media has shadow bans
and the MSM does have its slants
but they're subject to the laws of the land.
Your internet?
The wild west; say anything, get fans.
    (A posse grabbed by crafted lies. Stop following
    those www.hite rabbots down wonderland holes.)

It's seeds of truth that hook you in.
Though someone saying one thing valid,
like David Icke about speech freedom,
does not imply
that everything they say is certain
    ('I was right about current events decades ago, and
    I'm right about this, laugh all you like,' says a lizard
    meme on Icke's site.)

It wasn't ever any secret
that wealthy titans influence government.
But billionaires are not satanic
with reptile DNA.
It lets them off the hook, that otherment.
    (They fund lobbyists. Donate to parties. Hate unions.
    Make them accountable! They're not willing to share,
    or lose, their wealth or cede the control that comes
    with it, and if you had £3 billion you would be exactly
    like them unless you fought hard against the self-
    preserving, corruptible nature of being human.)

I have a tad of sympathy
for powerless folk at home and lonely;
unchallenging lives and no community.
I'm sorry you
got pulled in to this worldwide dodgy
    pyramid scheme. (But *actions have consequences*. It's
    not harmless. It's a new blueprint for industrial scale
    capture.)

To be so gullible can't be fun
but how do we forgive anyone
who finally took an interest in
current affairs
then put all their attention on
    a bunch of made-up hokum (in a land far, far away)?

FuQ for all the hours wasted
obsessing over the USA;
a screen-fuelled fever, tap-scroll mania.
It's so indulgent.
How come that is what made you pay
    attention? (Seduced by feeling privy to classified intel?)

The kind of folk who'd never demo'd
and found most politics a bore,
who possibly didn't bother to vote
then almost wiped
a congress out one winter morn.
    (January 6th was probably the most social contact
    many of those people'd had in a long time.)

It's maddening: to only worry
about child abuse when it's imaginary.
It's happening every helpless day
around our 'hoods,
not in the cellar of a pizza place.
    (My goodness, pizzerias are getting a bad rap lately
    what with HRC in DC and a genuine prince in Woking.)

If Q'ers are not short of time
to read and type, and to malign
then why not write to their own Prime
Minister
and make the case that they resign?
   (Or volunteer at a local youth centre or hold a bring-
   and-buy sale for Save the Children, sans hashtag.)

Sure, every truther has the right
to ask if a vaccine's safe to roll out.
Aye, have your David and Goliath fights
but based on facts.
If a jab has side-effects, shed more light
   (but don't bring microchips or mass sterilization
   into it.)

You want to fight some real corruption?
Avenge wrongs? Expose collusion?
Well pick your cause, there's plenty of them.
Your efforts would
be very welcome in stopping NHS
   erosion. (Campaigning for: a living rent, taxing the
   King, SNP transparency, rape conviction rates, or
   international agreements on data harvesting, safety
   for kids online, revenge porn or images stolen for
   deepfakes.)

Trump Jr. posted on the 'gram
a photo of Assange, Tate, Trump and Brand –
the DARVO kings. 'Notice a pattern?'
he asked. Yes,
that narcissists with difficult dads
     share a pathology for disregarding women's bodily
     autonomy. (Don Jr. 'doesn't believe in that much
     coincidence and neither should you.' I don't. It's
     clear: those men were not targeted for telling too
     much truth and Don Jr. knows that.)

Fresh whistles to the brainwashed flock.
The absence of a healthy gov
means they are letting you eat cake
and some are licking
the **crumbs** up. **Drops** from Q. Was who?
     (Most likely 8chan's operators – an army vet and his
     son, who'd left the US and owned a Japanese porn
     site – preaching to you about **patriotism** and **God**,
     come *on*, use your heads.)

So turn Q's tables back on him.
You always have to ask who is
telling me this? And why? What is
in it for them?
What is a cult? Who is worshipped?
     (That scheming muthafuQer. **Trust the plan? For God
     & country**? What about, Thou shalt not bear false
     witness?)

Now Q has gone but his army remains
to rally at the tug of their puppet strings
for MAGA, freedom convoys, a plandemic,
election fraud,
a climate hoax, or matrix witch
    hunts (or 5G, Putin, adrenochrome, moronic Omicron.)

Poor numpties you have all been played
mere chips in a silly nerd-boys' game.
The greatest con of nowadays.
Bamboozled sheeple
took the red pill but no Storm came.
    (But maybe yet Armageddon. The apophenic faithful
    primed and panting for a dramatic structural
    transformation.)

It's tragic that this idiotic
demented, banal utter bolloQs
is what could see off the rest of us.
Society –
as it has evolved over eons and epochs
    (of culture, philosophy, astronomy, medicine,
    technology – could all disappear when a bad actor's
    acolytes are whipped into a frenzied mob on
    Telegram over a concocted wrong, neighbour against
    neighbour, irrational, obedient foot soldiers enforcing
    a nascent dictatorship.)

Because how can we persuade the folks
who're inculcated and were told
to believe in nothing from before?
The ones who're sure
they've found real truth and now they *know*
   that everyone was lying to them (the WHO, the UN,
   newsreaders, their families. Who've decided that
   we're at war with a shady powerful cabal. How do we
   deprogram *them*? Oh nous, deliver us from this pish.)

If Q'ers want to reconsider
and turn their backs, we will be gentle.
With open arms, there'll be no ribbing.
Pandemic rules
sent lots of people loopy for a minute.
   (So let's regroup and reconnect. Democracy's on a
   shoogly peg. Irresponsibly, maliciously destabilized
   by **the biggest 'inside' 'approved' dump in American
   history**.)

The only Great Awakening
is realising that Q was a reckless villain
with a Pacific Time internet connection.
The only Sound
of Freedom is the signature jingle
   of an operating system as you log off from your devices.
   (Oh nous! It's desperate! Please come back!)

Found text source: https://qalerts.app/Q.pdf

About the Poets

Katie Ailes is a poet, researcher, producer, and educator focusing on performance poetry. She works as a producer with I Am Loud Productions and has co-devised and performed spoken word shows with them across the UK. Her poetry has been published widely and her poem 'Outwith' was chosen as one of the Scottish Poetry Library's Best of the Best Scottish Poems in 2019.

Craig Aitchison's poetry has featured in *Lallans, Nutmeg, Poetry Scotland* and on the Scottish Poetry Library website. He was awarded a New Writers' Award by the Scottish Book Trust for writing in Scots. In 2023 he won the Wigtown Prize for Scots Poetry and the Badenoch Poetry Competition.

Janette Ayachi – BA (Stirling University), MSc (Edinburgh University), is a Scottish-Algerian poet. She is a regular on BBC arts programmes and her first full poetry collection, *Hand Over Mouth Music* (Pavilion, LUP), won the Saltire Poetry Book of the Year Literary Award 2019. Her next book, *QuickFire, Slow Burning* (Pavilion), is released in 2024. www.janetteayachi.com.

Stephen Dornan is from Newtownards, County Down and lives in north-east Scotland, where he is a secondary teacher. He has published poetry in a number of journals and his collection, *The Jaa Banes*, appeared in 2020. He has also published academic pieces on Irish and Scottish writing in the age of Burns.

Roshni Gallgher is a poet from Leeds living in Edinburgh. Her debut pamphlet *Bird Cherry* is published by Verve Poetry Press. In 2022 she won an Edwin Morgan Poetry Award and a Scottish Book Trust New Writers Award. She writes about nature, memory, and silences. Find her at roshnigallagher.com.

Harry Josephine Giles is from Orkney and lives in Leith. Her poetry collections *The Games* (Out-Spoken, 2018) and *Tonguit* (Freight, 2015, republished by Stewed Rhubarb Press, 2018), were between them shortlisted for the Forward Prize for Best First Collection, the Saltire Prize and the Edwin Morgan Poetry Award. *Deep Wheel Orcadia* (Picador, 2021), an Orkney language science fiction verse novel, was a PBS Winter Recommendation and winner of the 2022 Arthur C. Clarke award.

W.N. Herbert is a Dundonian poet, academic and translator. He is Professor of Poetry and Creative Writing at Newcastle University, and has published widely with OUP, Arc, and others, including six books of poetry with Bloodaxe, several collaborative volumes with other poets, and numerous pamphlets.

David Kinloch was born, brought up and educated in Glasgow. The author of five full collections of poems, he is also a critic and scholar with many publications in the fields of French, Translation and Scottish Studies. He is a Trustee of The Edwin Morgan Trust and helped to set up the Scottish Writers' Centre.

Simon Lamb is a poet, performer and storyteller. He lives in Ayrshire where he is the Scriever, writer-in-residence at the Robert Burns Birthplace Museum, 2022–25. His poem 'The Working Birds' won the Robert Burns World Federation's Write a Habbie competition in 2021. His debut poetry collection is *A Passing On of Shells* (Scallywag Press, 2023), illustrated by former Children's Laureate Chris Riddell.

Iain Morrison is a poet, performer and programmer based in Edinburgh. His collection *I'm a Pretty Circler* (Vagabond Voices, 2018) was shortlisted for the Saltire Poetry Book of the Year Award in 2019. He trained as a musician and his practice moves between artforms, often ending up in a gallery.

Jeda Pearl is a Scottish Jamaican writer. Her poems and stories appear in art installations and several anthologies. In 2022, she was longlisted for the Women Poets' Prize and shortlisted for the Sky Arts RSL Award. Her debut poetry collection, *Time Cleaves Itself,* is forthcoming from Peepal Tree Press. Find her online: jedapearl.com • @JedaPearl.

Calum Rodger is a Glasgow-based poet and former academic turned software developer. His work explores the interfaces between poetics and technology, encompassing computer games, cinematic performance, handmade books and more besides. He is a former Scottish Slam Champion and holds a PhD in Scottish Literature. www.calumrodger.com.

Stewart Sanderson is a poet from Scotland. Three times shortlisted for the Edwin Morgan Poetry Award, he has also received an Eric Gregory Award, as well as Robert Louis Stevenson and Jessie Kesson Fellowships. Widely published in magazines and anthologies, his pamphlets *Fios* (2015) and *An Offering* (2018), and full-length collection *The Sleep Road* (2021) are published by Tapsalteerie.

Gill Shaw is a queer poet based in the Scottish Highlands where she balances writing with motherhood, lawyering and lecturing. Her debut pamphlet, *Touching Air*, was published by Stewed Rhubarb Press in April 2023. Gill runs monthly queer-friendly workshops to build community and celebrate diversity through poetry and spoken word.

Maria Sledmere is the author of over twenty books of poetry, including *An Aura of Plasma Around the Sun* (Hem Press, 2023), *Cocoa and Nothing* with Colin Herd (SPAM Press, 2023), *Visions & Feed* (HVTN Press, 2022), *String Feeling* (Erotoplasty Editions, 2022), and *The Luna Erratum* (Dostoyevsky Wannabe, 2021) – which was shortlisted for the Saltire Scottish Poetry Book of the Year 2022. She recently co-edited *The Last Song: Words for Frightened Rabbit* (Broken Sleep Books) with Aaron Kent. She is a Lecturer at the University of Strathclyde, a member of A+E Collective and managing editor of SPAM Press.

Taylor Strickland is the author of *Commonplace Book*, and *Dastram / Delirium*, winner of the 2023 Saltire Award for Scottish Poetry Book of the Year and a PBS Translation Choice. His work has appeared in *Poetry Wales*, *Poetry Northwest*, *New Statesman*, *TLS*, *Poetry Review*, and elsewhere. He lives in Glasgow with his wife, Lauren, and daughter, Eimhir.

Kate Tough's poem, 'People Made Glasgow', was selected as a Best Scottish Poem 2016 and her poetry pamphlet, *tilt-shift* (Tapsalteerie, 2016), was runner up in the 2017 CMMA. Since then she's been shortlisted for the Wigtown Prize under a pen name, and was invited to participate in The Edwin Morgan Trust's International Translation Workshop, Stanza and Return To Form. Her short stories are collected in *Kissing Lying Down* (Picón, 2022), after appearing in *The Brooklyn Review*, *The Texas Review* and other journals. www.katetough.com

www.tapsalteerie.co.uk

Tapsalteerie is an award-winning poetry publishing house
based in rural Aberdeenshire. We produce an eclectic range
of publications with a focus on new poets, translation,
collaborations and innovative writing.